D1499006

TIM & NINA

WE LOOK FORWARD TO
HELPING YOU EVERY STEP
OF THE WAY ON THIS
JOURNEY THROUGH RETIREMENT.

WINNING IN RETIREMENT

WINNING

— IN —

RETIREMENT

WHEN EVERY DAY
IS **SATURDAY**

CHAD SLAGLE

BIG CAT PUBLISHING

COPYRIGHT © 2020 CHAD SLAGLE

All rights reserved.

WINNING IN RETIREMENT
When Every Day Is Saturday

ISBN   978-1-5445-0696-8 *Hardcover*
978-1-5445-0694-4 *Paperback*
978-1-5445-0695-1 *Ebook*

To my wife April, and our children, G-Money, Mae, Huddy, and Bear. Thank you for being on this journey with me.

CONTENTS

INTRODUCTION

WHEN EVERY DAY IS SATURDAY

Twenty years ago, most Americans preparing to retire did not need to do much financial planning because there was already a plan, called a **pension**, put together for you by your employer. It was a defined benefit plan where you worked for twenty, thirty, or forty years, and they took a little money out of your paycheck every period and put it aside. When you retired, that was your income stream, and the only decision you had to make was to either take 100 percent for yourself or to make sure your spouse was taken care of if something happened to you before him or her.

Once you made your decision, you knew that you would have that guaranteed income each and every month for the rest of your life, and your spouse's life, no matter how long either of you lived. From there, you simply adjusted your lifestyle to match the level of income you knew to expect.

Today, however, it is a very different story. According to the Pension Rights Center, **less than 20 percent of American workers have a pension.** And that number is going down.

It's a scary thing to retire in the twenty-first century. You don't know if you're going to live to be 75, 85, or 105. If you're like many of the families we work with, you're worried that the money you've saved won't be enough. You don't know if you'll be able to retire on time. There's a lot of anxiety all around.

Another major concern for retirees today, of course, is long-term care. What happens if you get sick and have to spend months or even years in a long-term care facility? How will you pay those bills?

What we've seen, over and over again, is that when you build a *game plan*, all those fears start to subside. Even the body language changes: Shoulders relax. Faces brighten. Ultimately, you develop a peace of mind, knowing you have a structured plan in place. You feel confident you will be taken care of—no matter how many years you end up living.

WHAT IS A SUCCESSFUL RETIREMENT?

When people come to our workshops, one of the questions we always ask them is "What day of the week do you spend the most money?" For almost everyone who is still working, the answer is the same: Saturday.

It makes sense. Mondays through Fridays—the weekdays—are also *work*days. There just isn't that much time outside of work to spend money. You wake up, go to work, come home, make dinner, and maybe watch some TV. Then you go to bed, wake up, and do it all over again. When the end of the week comes, you want to have a little fun. Saturdays are when families tend to do things like go to restaurants, movies, concerts, and sporting events, as well as shopping and running errands.

When you *retire*, however, there's no distinction between workdays and non-work days. That's right, folks: in retirement **every day is Saturday.**

How are you going to afford it, and even more fundamentally, what are you going to *do* with all that free time?

It's no longer the norm to sit in a rocking chair on your front porch and get old. Think about your lifestyle. Do you want to have a second home in Florida or Arizona? Are there hobbies you want to spend more time doing, like hunting, fishing, cycling, or gardening? Is there a club or volunteer organization you want to belong to? Is it your dream to play golf at all the nicest courses in the United States? Or maybe you want to travel across the country in an RV or take your entire family on one big trip every year.

Then the big question becomes: what income do you need to support that lifestyle?

Often, retirees haven't given much thought to their lifestyle goals; nor do they know how long their money will last. We find that a lot of our clients have just been sitting on their money and not spending it because they're afraid of running out.

That is why it's so crucial to define your lifestyle and build a written, structured game plan to support that lifestyle.

A JOURNEY, NOT A DESTINATION

We hear it from many of the people we work with: after they retired, they felt like they had no purpose in life, almost like a postretirement hangover. This is not surprising when you think about it: retirement is a massive life change, one of the biggest transitions we go through as humans.

Say you're a foreman or a boss. For all these years, you've had people looking up to you. You've been responsible for leading them. Now, all of a sudden, you're retired and there's no one for you to lead. You've lost your identity.

For so many of us, our job is the thing that keeps us going, day after day. It's only natural, then, that there would be a lot of anxiety and discomfort when it all comes to an end and we retire from our jobs.

But what if, instead of retiring *from* your job, you could retire *to* something else—something new and meaningful?

You may have another twenty-five, thirty, thirty-five years left! What do you want to *do* with that time? It may seem like common sense, but most people don't think this way. They've worked so hard their whole life just to get to this point. Their focus has been on getting *to* retirement, not *through* it. Now they're finally here; they've made it—but they don't know what to actually do with this thing they've been longing for all these years! Often, they grow lonely. They feel like they don't have a reason to get out of bed in the morning.

This is why it's so important to understand that **retirement is a journey, not a destination.** And in order to do that, you have to have a game plan to retire *to* your ideal retirement, not simply *from* the workforce.

Our happiest clients have a clear vision of what they want

in retirement. Some wish to travel; others play golf, or fish, or hunt. The point is: they know what they want their lives to look like and they are excited to make it happen. But in order to achieve their goal of retiring *to* that new life, obviously they have to have the necessary funds available and secure to be able to pursue those hobbies and perform those activities.

That's where we come in and help you **build a plan.**

YOUR RETIREMENT GPS

Once you have a clear vision of where you want to go, we use our four-step guided planning system to help get you there. It's just like when you get into your car: you know the location you're trying to get to, and you probably have some idea of where it is, but you don't know exactly how to find it. So you punch the address into your GPS system, and it tells you turn-by-turn what roads to take, what turns to make.

When I was a kid, my family took one big trip every summer, and we all looked forward to it. My parents, brother, sister, and I would load up the family station wagon and make the two-hour trek to Busch Stadium in St. Louis to watch our beloved St. Louis Cardinals. And even though we made the drive every year, my dad would still get lost every single time. My mom would have the map in her lap, but it made no difference. He would have to make at least two or three stops at local gas stations along the way to ask for directions because when the map failed, there was no backup plan.

You may think that your 401(k) or company plan is your perfectly planned map for retirement, but retirement today is different, just as navigation today is different than it was twenty or thirty years ago. Today we have a GPS system that will guide us turn by turn until we reach our destination. Thirty years ago, stopping at gas stations was the way a lot of people got to unfamiliar places, and pensions alone got retirees through retirement. Things are constantly changing. Pensions are rare in today's workforce and company plans cannot be counted on to get you successfully through retirement...unless you have a plan that goes along with them.

Which, again, is where we come in. Tell us what lifestyle you want to have, what hobbies, and how much income you're going to need to have coming in to support that lifestyle. We then use that information to guide you, turn-by-turn, step-by-step, showing you what vehicles to use to get there and how to navigate your successful retirement, start to finish.

We show you **HOW TO WIN.**

WINNING IN RETIREMENT

If you are reading this book, chances are you are experiencing some anxiety around your retirement. You're afraid to spend your money because you fear it might run out.

Well, I am here to tell you: **you are going to be okay.** As long as you are smart about it and have a set game plan in place, your money can and will last the rest of your life.

Recently, we had clients come in who wanted to buy a second home in The Villages near Orlando, Florida. But they were fearful that if they spent that money on the new house, they wouldn't have enough left to last them through their retirement years. In reality, they had plenty of money. The problem was that it was almost all invested in the market. When your money is in stocks, you have no idea how long it's going to last. You don't know how long you're going to live or if the market is going to go up or down.

So, in the case of these particular clients, we sat down with them, discussed their lifestyle goals, what kind of income they would need if they bought the second property—and then built a game plan for them. They walked out of our office knowing exactly what income they would need to support their lifestyle, including both their first and second home. And because we had this game plan, our clients were assured that the necessary funds would be coming in each and every month for the rest of their lives, no matter how long they lived.

You too can have this clarity and peace of mind. You can win in retirement and not have to be kept up at night worrying about running out of money.

It may be hard to see now, but there is a light at the end of the tunnel; I promise you. Maybe you are also considering a major purchase, a second home or something else, and fretting about whether your money will last. Obviously, as with everything in life, the devil is in the details. But in general, if you have the right game plan in place, it is very likely that you can, indeed, make the purchase—and you will still be okay and have your money last you through the rest of your life.

In fact, even if you have already made mistakes in retirement, it's not too late. As I have learned in my own life, mistakes happen—the key is to learn from them, as well as from the mistakes of others.

> "Too many of us are not living our dreams because we are living our fears."
>
> —LES BROWN

WHO AM I?

I am a little different than most financial advisors. I grew up in a small town in Central Illinois, working on a farm. In this way, I am very much like a lot of the clients I see. I come from a blue-collar background. That's where I got my work ethic. In fact, **everything I learned about business was learned on a farm or in a locker room.** I grew up playing football and went on to coach high-school football at a very high level—and drew from those experiences in building my practice, Slagle Financial. It's also how my team and I create successful retirement outcomes for our clients: we sit down with you and put together a good structured "game plan" for winning.

The way it works is this. First, we create clarity on what you want to accomplish in retirement. Then, we analyze your risks, as well as any fees you may currently be paying. Finally, we implement a plan of action to fill the gaps between where you are now and where you want to be.

Through this approach and process, we have helped count-less families make the most of their money for the rest of their lives—and go from a state of anxiety, or sometimes even despair, to the peace of mind that comes with a happy, comfortable retirement that is also genuinely exciting and rewarding.

You can have this too. But it all begins with getting clear on what you want your own retirement to look like.

PART ONE

—

CREATING YOUR PLAN

My parents, Ron and Linda Slagle, are two of the hardest working people I know. Throughout my life, they have taught me so many valuable lessons—about responsibility, perseverance, and much more.

My parents have always lived in a small town, and love gardening, going to local sporting events, and spending time with family. Because of this, they never really thought about planning for retirement. They have always lived a life that they love.

Now in their mid-seventies, my parents still have to work to ensure there's enough extra money coming in—beyond their modest Social Security income—to make ends meet and support their lifestyle. They still run a full paper route every single morning, rain or shine, 365 days a year. They still raise chickens to sell the eggs. My mother is also still the town librarian. Their modest life doesn't include yearly Florida vacations or Alaskan cruises, but like I said, they live a life that they love.

Once I left the small farm town I grew up in, I realized that retirement can be anything you want it to be. It can be an exciting new chapter of life if you put in the work and create a plan for that life. Many people retire and begin exploring the world or checking lifelong dreams off their bucket lists.

My parents are from a different generation. The only way

they knew to get ahead was through work, work, and more work. They didn't ask anybody for anything and were determined to make a life for themselves. The only way my parents knew to get ahead in life was to work *harder*. I admire that about them, but if I am being honest, I would like my retirement to be filled with less work and more leisure.

To put that another way, my parents live to work, like their parents before them. They spent their whole lives working—it was all they knew. My mother's side of the family were all farmers, and as farmers, they worked until they couldn't work anymore. It was the same on my father's side. His family ran a restaurant in the small farm town of Winchester, Illinois, where I grew up. But, like in a lot of small towns, eventually the economy dried up. There was simply not enough clientele to continue with the restaurant. Also, my father ran the business with my grandmother, and she got to be too old to take care of it. When I was about fourteen or fifteen, the family sold the restaurant. My dad had to work at a meat-processing plant until he was able to retire. But, as we have seen, "retirement" didn't actually mean not working. Both sides of my family worked to pay the bills. Whatever they had, they spent. They really didn't save much for retirement. My grandmother didn't even have any life insurance. This way of living was carried down to the next generation: my grandparents didn't have a plan for retirement (virtually no one from their era did)—and so then neither did my parents.

I am writing this book so that no other retirees have to enter retirement without a plan. When you retire, you should be able to fully close the door on working and enter a brand new chapter of life.

Instead of "living to work," I want everyone who reads this to embrace the idea of working to live.

> I want everyone who reads this to embrace the idea of *working to live.*

This means working to make money so that you can live the life you want outside of work. It means living the lifestyle you've always dreamed of once you retire.

Work so you can live.

But in order to retire happily and comfortably, you have to make some changes, be open to new ideas—and commit to building a plan.

It all begins with **creating clarity**. Why are you working? When you retire, what do you want your life to look like? What kind of dreams do you have? Again, if you're like many of today's retirees, you think about your future as retiring *from* something. In the following chapters, I call on you to shift your mindset and think about it instead as retiring *to* something. But what that "something" might be is different for each individual and each family.

In order to figure out what exactly it is that *you* want to retire to—the subject of part 1—you need to create clarity, beginning with answering the question: what do you want your *lifestyle* to look like in retirement? Then: how much income are you going to need coming in to support that lifestyle? If you can come to clarity on these items, you will be on your way to building a great plan for protecting and preserving your savings—as well as the peace of mind that comes with knowing your retirement is secure.

> When you retire, you are not just retiring **from** your job, you are retiring **to** the lifestyle you've always dreamed of.

CHAPTER 1

WHAT ARE YOUR CONCERNS?

"If it doesn't challenge you, it won't change you."

—FRED DEVITO

Not only are people living so much longer today, but there is also more uncertainty in the market. If you're like many retirees, and you have all your money sitting in the stock market, you now have two problems to contend with. Is that money going to last you through the rest of your life? You have no idea, because, one, you don't know how long you're going to live, and two, you don't know what's going to happen in the market. Both are unknown variables.

In today's world, there are many, many things out there that fall outside of our control and give us anxiety.

For example, twenty years ago we had a national economy, but today we have a global economy. So when China, Europe, or Greece have problems in their economy, even though you may not have money invested in those countries, it will still bring your portfolio down, and you'll lose money. Similarly, we cannot control what happens with the natural disasters that affect our economy: the tsunamis, fires, earthquakes, and droughts. Heck, we can hardly even control our own government, other than the vote that you and I have every few years.

So what *can* we control?

A lot. We can control how our money is invested, what our money is invested in, and who we choose to work with when it comes to investing our hard-earned dollars.

That is why it's so important at this stage in the game to plan for the worst and hope for the best. You need to start right away by insulating your portfolio from a downturn in the market.

> Plan for the worst and hope for the best.

WHY WE BEHAVE THE WAY WE DO

Behavioral economics shows us that when the market goes up or down, we react with emotion and not with logic.

When the market is down, we start freaking out and putting our money on the sidelines, and when the market is up, we pump more money in. The problem with that, of course, is that when the market does come back up, we lose out on the ability to benefit from the upswing. We lose because we're behaving reactively rather than proactively.

It doesn't make matters any easier that we live in an era of oversaturation. We get so much information from so many different places. We go to a workshop and they tell us to do this or that with our money. We watch the news and they tell us another thing. Then we go to our financial advisor, who tells us something completely different. Then we read an article online or in a newspaper, which then puts entirely new ideas in our head.

What ends up happening is that, even though we know we need to make a plan or make changes in our portfolio, we don't act on that knowledge at all. Instead, we get what's called **decision paralysis.**

Why do we act this way when it comes to investing our hard-earned dollars? Because we are humans, driven by emotions like fear and greed. Like it or not, these instincts drive us, and they drive our money.

This is just one of the many things you need to understand about the new world we live in before you can even start to look at your lifestyle goals and build an appropriate retire-ment plan.

There are so many options when it comes to retiring today, and it can be hard to figure out what is best for you. Take the time now to educate yourself—so that you can win.

ARE YOU GOING TO BE OKAY?

When all is said and done, what retirees today *really* care about, what they really want to know, is whether they're going to be okay or not. Are they going to run out of money? Will their money last them through the rest of their life? Do they even have enough to retire? What's the magic number?

I hear it all the time: "When can I retire? How much do I need? Will my money last throughout retirement?"

Then they want to know about Social Security. When should they start drawing Social Security?

Finally, there is the unknown of long-term care. Are they going to get sick? And if they do get sick, how are they going to pay the bills? Where's that money going to come from?

What about *their* parents? Taking care of aging parents is much more common these days because the elder genera-tion doesn't have the money to be able to pay for a nursing home. Moreover, many retirees are still simultaneously trying to care for their kids, still loaning their kids money. These retirees are described as being part of the "**sandwich generation**": On one side they're taking care of their children and on the other, their parents—when what they really need to be doing is taking care of themselves!

No wonder there is so much anxiety around retirement.

> The "sandwich generation" refers to middle-aged adults (often in their forties and fifties) who are caring for both elderly parents and their own children (Investopedia).

I remember one particular gentleman who attended our Empower University, which is a two-day educational course we hold at colleges throughout the area. He was so nervous about his money that, when I called him up to the podium to help me with an exercise, he couldn't stop sweating. Having gotten to know him since, I came to see even more of his anxiety around money. Anytime my team and I made a financial suggestion, he would bombard us with emails because he was so unsure and felt like his situation was so precarious. At the age of sixty-two, he couldn't stop worrying about the possibility that he might get laid off from his job. If he did, he wondered, would he and his spouse have enough money to last them the rest of their lives?

As it turns out, this fellow has $650,000 sitting in his 401(k), and his wife has another $150,000 in hers. Their goal is for him to retire in five years and her in ten. At the college class, he wanted to know if he and his wife could afford to have a second home in Park City, Utah. I was determined to figure this out for him. So we talked further and put a game plan together. Ultimately, we made him see that he and his wife *could*, in fact, afford the second home, even *if* he got laid off.

That's right: even if he were to lose his job, he would still have a healthy income stream from a combination of his investments, Social Security, and a small pension. Working with us, he was able to set enough money aside to put a down payment on a condo in Park City, as well as make sure there was enough to cover everything that he and his wife needed to live when they retired.

That, in short, is what we're able to do for our clients—and it's what we are sharing with you now in this book.

It's a very scary thing when you retire today. You don't know if you're going to live to be 75, 85, or 105. How can you know if your money is going to last you through the rest of your life?

We don't know how long you are going to live, but we do know how to make your money last as long as you do.

When our clients leave our office, they are visibly lighter.

That is how we hope *you* feel after reading this book: more comfortable and at ease because you now have a structured, set plan that will work for you—no matter how many more years you may live.

It's a remarkable transformation. Our clients often go from being scared of spending their money—and living out their dreams, like buying that second home at the lake, on the beach, or in the mountains—to having full confidence and peace of mind, knowing that they *can*, in fact, win in retirement, and in a way that's not risky.

CHAPTER 2

WHAT IS YOUR PERFECT RETIREMENT?

"A goal without a plan is just a wish."

—ANTOINE DE SAINT-EXUPÉRY

Twenty years ago retirees really didn't have to do much financial planning, because when they retired, they automatically had a pension plan set up. Today, however, less than 20 percent of American workers have a pension, and that number is dropping each year. So **now the responsibility is all on the individual.** I don't say this to scare you. It doesn't mean financial planning has to be grueling. But it does mean you have to be proactive. The days of depending on your employer and the government are gone. The burden is now all on you, the retiree.

Living in a pensionless society means that when you retire, it's *as if* you're experiencing twenty-five to thirty-five years of unemployment! Behind these numbers lies one of the biggest concerns of retirees today: how they're going to make their money last. They may have a fairly significant lump sum sitting in their 401(k), but they're still scared—because now they've got to make sure that money doesn't run out over the coming years and even decades.

> The days of depending on your employer and the government are gone. The burden is now all on YOU, the retiree.

In chapter 1, we learned about the fears and anxieties that so many retirees face. One of the biggest issues we see is that our clients are in the dark when it comes to their investments—the reason being that although they have 401(k)s, profit-sharing plans, or company plans at work, they are given very little financial education around these programs. They may see a 401(k) administrator or human resources once every six months, or there may be a website to visit. But even though they're putting 10 to 15 percent of their annual salaries toward their retirement plans, they really have no idea how these plans actually work, what they're investing in, or what the long-term consequences are if they don't invest properly.

Moreover, a lot of people don't realize until they get to the point of retiring just how daunting it can all be if they're not on top of it. Suddenly, they're confronted with the realization that their money has to last them throughout the rest of their life.

But knowledge is power, and **figuring out what you actually want out of your retirement—getting it all down on paper—is the first step to freedom.**

When we sit down with a new client in our office, in our initial information-gathering session, we ask them about their risk tolerance, their income needs, their lifestyle goals, their family dynamics, their liabilities and assets—and part of those assets are their investments.

How much money are they willing to lose? How much money do they need to support their lifestyle, hobbies, and possibly their retirement goals? Do they need money to support their parents or children? Do they own their home?

All in all, we help them to start educating themselves. Creating clarity for the client means, fundamentally, opening their eyes to how very important planning for retirement is. We talk about their lifestyle and how they want to maintain it, and we emphasize the need for them to learn and empower themselves, starting right then and there.

DEFINE YOUR EXPECTED LIFESTYLE

All of our clients share a similar sentiment when they come in: they wonder if they have enough money to retire. Of course, that all depends on what kind of lifestyle they're accustomed to or what lifestyle they want to have during retirement. That is why we ask so many questions about their vision for retirement.

Before you can build your plan or blueprint for a successful retirement, you need to create clarity around some basic questions: Why are you working? When you get to retirement, what do you want your life to look like? What kind of dreams do you have? What are your hobbies? What do you like to do now? What keeps you busy when you're not working?

As we've already talked about, most retirees today are retiring *from* their job, not *to* a new chapter of life, a new adventure.

If you don't have any hobbies, you should try to find some! You have to think about what's going to keep you going, keep you motivated, and give you a reason to live, once you retire.

At Slagle Financial, we have a program called Retire Together, which is designed to foster community. We formed this with our clients because we saw all the fun they had at our events and recognized how much they had in common, being in the same walk of life. Retire Together gives these families a digital platform to connect with one another, discuss their hobbies, and even plan trips or golf outings together.

When you retire, it's easy to lose some of those human bonds, both professional and social, that you've felt in the past and have maybe taken for granted. In particular, a lot of our clients say they've lost that sense of camaraderie and they want to find it again. To help them with this, we hold four or five Retire Together events each year—and from there, people go off and form their own groups together: travel groups, book clubs, and more.

These are the kinds of activities that make up what I call your "mental lifestyle." When you think about what kind of life you want to have in retirement, you definitely need to factor in those mental aspects. One of the hardest parts of retiring can be the feelings of loneliness and isolation. Find things to do that get you out of the house and around other people.

You also need to factor in the physical: there are many ways to prioritize your health in retirement. Pick up some healthy hobbies like walking, running, hiking, or cycling. Many health insurance programs, including Medicare Supplement, cover gym fees to encourage people to stay healthy—so make sure to look into that. If you're exercising and staying in shape, you're going to have a much more enjoyable retirement than if you're just sitting around eating at buffet diners all the time. And you're probably going to live longer!

When my client Jim stopped working, he struggled with his lack of purpose postretirement. In his job, he had been a boss, managing a small team that ran the computer system for a racetrack. But once he retired, he wasn't in a leadership role anymore. Part of his identity was missing. He had to search for his new purpose, and he did so by focusing on all of the things he had hoped to do in his life but never had time for when he was working: home renovations, woodworking, and the freedom to travel whenever and wherever.

His wife Susan felt that she initially didn't have a purpose in retirement but came to realize her passion for volunteering in the community. She is now involved in multiple organizations and even sits on the board of one. She has found a purpose in her passions in retirement.

I am happy to report that both Jim and Susan are enjoying the heck out of their retirement. They both stay busy, active, and inspired, each with their own things that make them happy and fulfilled. Like a lot of our clients, what they wanted was simple:

- An income stream that would never run out
- A purpose, meaning, or reason to get out of bed every morning
- The financial freedom to do whatever they wanted in retirement

> What do you want your lifestyle to look like in retirement? How much income do you need coming in to be able to support that lifestyle?

DEFINE YOUR RISK

After looking at your lifestyle, you need to ask yourself some crucial questions about your risk tolerance. How much of your money that you have invested are you willing to lose? Can you lose 10 to 20 percent? How comfortable are you with the stock market?

If you are not willing to take any risks, you may not have the growth potential you need for your perfect retirement. On the other hand, if you are taking too much risk, you stand to lose a lot of your portfolio, which could threaten your lifestyle.

That's why it's so important to get specific here: How much are you willing to lose in a down market? What **rate of return** do you expect from your investments?

What income do you need now? If the answer now is none, when *will* you need it—and how much?

Many of the clients we encounter do not have a written retirement income plan. This is probably the most important thing to have going into retirement. A written retirement income plan shows exactly how much your money in retirement will provide in monthly income, each and every month for the rest of your life and the rest of your spouse's life. It doesn't matter what happens in the market; it doesn't matter what happens with interest rates. This plan is solid proof that your money can and will last. You may tell yourself that you already have that all planned out, but make sure you have it all *written down*, not just planned out in your mind.

It is also extremely important to know what you are paying in fees. Many people who walk into our offices have no idea how much they're paying in fees. We cannot stress this enough: **educate yourself on the fees you are paying and why you are paying them.** (Much more to come on this in part 2.)

To be clear, when we talk this way about our clients and their lack of education around these matters, it's not to criticize them. Rather, we are trying to get across just how very important it is to work with an advisor who can help you eliminate unnecessary risks.

Even if you already do have a written retirement plan, an advisor can help you, for example, to make sure that the plan takes into consideration the rate of inflation and cost of living.

And it's not just any advisor that you need, but the *right* advisor. If you're like a lot of retirees out there, you have somebody from your 401(k) plan who calls you every six months and talks to you. Or maybe you have a financial advisor who sees you once a year. But you have to ask yourself: Does this person give you all the advice you need to know if you're on track or not? Do they make you confident that you're not taking on too much risk and that you're going to have an income stream to last the rest of your life and your spouse's life?

We talked recently to a husband and wife who are big St. Louis Cardinals fans. After they attended our workshop, they wanted to meet with us for a complimentary consultation. When this couple retired, they had about $750,000 in their portfolio, but all of it was sitting in the stock market, and they were concerned about taking too much risk. They also didn't know what they were paying in fees on their accounts.

But one thing they knew for sure: they loved their baseball team and wanted to spend three months every year in Jupiter, Florida, watching the Cardinals in spring training.

It was what gave them the most happiness and pleasure. But to do so on an ongoing basis would require an extra $15,000 per year of income.

In their case, we took them through our process to create clarity, found out what they wanted, put together an evaluation, broke down their fees, and showed them the risk.

Ultimately, we were able to lower their fees by 50 percent and get them to the proper safe-risk ratio. This meant there was enough money set aside that was secure, and not at risk, to find the extra income needed to spend those three months a year in Florida and buy a condo there.

KNOW YOUR BUDGET

When we talk about your perfect retirement, we're talking not just about your lifestyle but also, of course, your budget. Unfortunately, a lot of people today don't live on a budget at all. They just adjust their lifestyle to the income they receive. But as you get closer to retirement, you absolutely need to think about your budget.

There is an old rule of thumb that says that in retirement, you should have 70 to 80 percent of your pre-retirement income coming in. I don't agree with this. When you retire, **every day is Saturday** and you need *just as much* income, or even more, as you did before you retired.

Knowing your budget means knowing how much income you have to have right now, as a working person. What is that money going toward (your bills, your travel, your everyday living expenses)?

Then, it's about **knowing your number.**

What does it mean to "know your number"? Let's say that when you retire, you want an extra $2,000 to $4,000 a month. You know that the overall amount you're going to need per month after you retire is about $10,000, and your pension and Social Security will only pay $6,000; that means you have a $4,000 per month "**shortfall.**"

A shortfall, according to Investopedia, is "an amount by which a financial obligation or liability exceeds the required amount of cash that is available."

Where is that money going to come from? You have to make sure you have enough in other 401(k)s, IRAs, retirement accounts, or your own personal savings to cover the shortfall every month for the rest of your life, whether you live to be 85, 95, or 105.

So, when we say "know your number," we're talking about the amount you *have to have*—the shortfall that must come from your retirement accounts and personal investments to be able to support your lifestyle.

Know your number to find your shortfall.

WHAT COMES NEXT

Now that you have created clarity around your lifestyle and your budget, and how much income you need to have coming in (taking into consideration your family dynamics, liabilities, and assets), you can begin to lay the foundation for building a game plan toward that perfect retirement.

You're not there yet, but you're on your way. Finally, you're taking charge and putting yourself in the driver's seat of your own future.

Now you need to figure out where exactly you stand in terms of your perfect retirement, where you are currently on track, and where you are off track and need to make a change.

PART TWO

—

GETTING ON
TRACK

When I started my practice back in 1995, I was only twenty-two years old. I was very green and had a lot to learn, but I knew I could succeed by being sincere and following my instincts. Every time I sat in front of a prospective client, I would ask myself, "Is this what I would recommend to my grandma?" If the answer was yes, I would go ahead and make the recommendation.

Then, in my early thirties, after being in the business for about ten years and having seen some success, I would look at my clients as if I were working with my *parents*. I would ask myself, "Is this what I would recommend to Mom and Dad?"

Now, at age forty-six, with my oldest son Grayson in his first year of college and my youngest daughter Nola about to turn eleven, for the first time in my life I look at my clients and see *myself* in their shoes. I am starting to think about what retirement looks like for my wife April and me. We are having conversations about what our life together will be in ten years, when the kids are all out of the house. What kind of income stream will we need to have coming in when we are empty nesters?

What are our goals? What kind of lifestyle do we want to have? For the last eighteen years, our lives have revolved around our children, and it has been nothing short of amazing—the best adventure ever. Now, however, we must think about what comes next. How will we fill our time when we are not driving from one kid's sports game to the next? Do we want to travel to all the destinations on our bucket list, or buy a second home in Florida or Arizona, or chase around our grandchildren like we did our children? Maybe all of the above!

It can be very exciting to think this way, but it can also be scary wondering if you have enough money to stop doing what you've done for the past thirty to forty years—to not work anymore and be confident that you'll still have enough money coming in to last you for the rest of your life.

So many of us think about that retirement date and become laser-focused on the idea of finally doing it, retiring from our work or job. But we neglect to consider what we are retiring *to*.

> When you retire, it's not the beginning of the end. It's a new beginning.

The next twenty to thirty years can either be a very exciting time or a depressing time. It all comes down to planning and preparation.

In the following chapters, we will show you exactly what you need to know to build your perfect retirement plan.

CHAPTER 3

WHAT TRACK ARE YOU ON?

"We don't have to be smarter than the rest. We have to be more disciplined than the rest."

—WARREN BUFFETT

One of the issues we discuss with our clients is what phase of life they're in. **There are three financial phases we all have in our lives.**

The first phase of your financial life is what we call the **accumulation phase.** It starts at about age twenty, when you start working, and the whole goal of this phase is to work long enough and save up enough money so that eventually you'll get to the point, around age sixty, when you can retire.

During the accumulation phase, if you're, say, in your forties and lose 30 to 40 percent of your portfolio—which happened to a lot of people back in 2008—yes it's a big deal, but not catastrophic. You still have another twenty years at least to make up for those losses.

You have *new money* coming in, whether from a salary or an hourly wage. No doubt it stinks to lose 10, 20, or 30 percent of your portfolio, but the new money coming in helps make up for those losses.

When you get to your late fifties or early sixties, however, you enter the **preservation phase** of life. This is the point at which you retire and no longer have earnings coming in. Now if you lose 30 to 40 percent of your portfolio, it's a big deal because you don't have that new money to make up for the losses. You also have less time—and in today's pensionless society, you may need to draw from that money to live off of.

Which brings us to the third and final phase, the **distribution phase**. At this point, most people want to take what they've accumulated and make sure it lasts throughout the rest of their life. When they do decide to walk out on life, they want to make sure it's passed on to their children, grandchildren, churches, or whoever their beneficiaries may be, in the most tax-efficient and tax-advantageous manner.

WHAT DO YOU WANT MONEY TO DO FOR YOU?

I think we can all agree we want our money to *grow*.

Hopefully, if our money grows, we're going to have a lot of dividends or interest.

We also want our money to *last*. We have no idea how long we are going to live, but we know that we want our money to stay safe throughout our entire life (not our *life expectancy*). This is called "safety of principal" or "preservation of capital."

What does safety mean to *you*? It's different for everybody. If you have a 401(k) at work, you're probably used to questions like "If the market dropped 10 percent, how would you feel?" Basically, what this question is trying to get at is your risk tolerance.

For someone who is already retired, the answer to this question is likely different than for someone still working. In fact, I had a widow come to my office for a complimentary consultation, and when I asked her what safety meant to her, she took out her brokerage statement, placed it in front of me, and said, "Safety means that three months from now, when I get my next statement and open it up, I want to make sure I have the same or more money."

Safe money, or safety of principal, is what you have when

your principal is protected from loss. But you must follow certain guidelines. If you don't want to lose money, you have to educate yourself on what your accounts will do in an economic downturn. When you put your money into a stock or mutual fund, what is the worst-case scenario? If you do decide to take your money out and go somewhere else, what will leaving early cost you?

In order to get your money to grow in today's market, you can't just take it and throw it into a CD. You would be lucky to make 1 percent on that. To get your money to grow, you have to put it in the stock market. The problem with the stock market, of course, is that you have no control over what happens in it!

There are things you *can* control when it comes to investing your hard-earned dollars that you've spent a whole lifetime creating: *how* your money is invested, *what* it's invested in, and *who* you choose to work with.

Get these three things right and your money will grow *and* last.

> You can't control what happens in the stock market, but you *can* control how your money is invested, what it's invested in, and who you choose to work with.

What *else* do you want your money to do for you? You've worked your entire life to earn this money; now it's time to make your money work for you.

In order to *spend* your money, it's got to be liquid.

The problem, again, is that you have no idea how long you're going to live. How can you set a game plan to get yourself through the rest of your life when you don't know how long you need that money to last? This may seem obvious, but it's super important. If you don't have a pension or an income stream set up, you may find yourself in trouble.

Many of us also want our money to create a *legacy* and be passed down to our loved ones. We want to be able to leave something to our kids and/or grandkids.

Even if this desire doesn't resonate strongly with you, I'm sure you would rather be able to choose where your money goes after you're gone—maybe to your church or whoever your beneficiaries may be—than have it just get funneled to the IRS or a nursing home.

Knowing what you want your money to do for you is key to getting on the right track with your retirement plan.

But then you must also look at how much *risk* you're taking.

DO YOU HAVE THE RIGHT ADVISOR FOR YOUR RETIREMENT?

When it comes to financial planning, most advisors today are focusing only on the accumulation and growth of your money. But when you get closer to retirement, you have different priorities: you want to make sure you are working with an advisor who is an expert in the areas of preservation and distribution.

We meet with a lot of people who are completely naked in the stock market. They have no stop-loss, no covered calls, no hedge funds. Why have they left themselves exposed and vulnerable in this way? It's because they sat down with an advisor who has no clue about preservation.

The reason most financial advisors are focused only on growth and not preservation is because of their own structural incentives.

Financial planning, simply put, is making sure that the path you are on is leading you to the destination you want. Many of you are reading this book because you fear you're on the wrong path and want to see if there's a better way. There is.

Finding the correct retirement path for yourself can make a huge difference: providing consistent returns on your retirement money (without the fear of loss ever again); keeping the IRS's hands off of your family's money (now and in the future); and leaving money to your heirs for generations to come. In the next few chapters, I am going to show you how to get on a retirement path that can help you accomplish all of these things.

There are also vehicles you set up when you're still in your accumulation phase, still working—the 401(k)s, 403(b)s, and other retirement accounts. Those are good vehicles for investing money to get you to retirement. The problem is, if you don't adjust your portfolio for your correct stage of life, the vehicles that got you to retirement may be the same vehicles that blow you up in retirement.

But many advisors won't tell you that because they only work in one world, the Wall Street world (more on that in the next chapter).

As you approach retirement, you want to make sure you're working with an advisor who's insulating your portfolio from a downturn in the market—because that's what's most important today.

Find an advisor that you can trust.

If the market were to have a 20 to 30 percent correction in the next year, with the way your portfolio is set up right now, how much would you lose? Are you in a place where you can bounce back? Or are you naked in the stock market?

You need to **stress-test** your portfolio to figure this out. A stress test is a computer-simulated technique to analyze how investments fare in possible future situations and drastic economic scenarios (Investopedia).

Look, we're not telling you that you should *never* take risks. But you need to educate yourself and know what the numbers are. A stress test will give you that information, tell you what kind of risk you're taking, and also what you're paying in fees...the wholesale price or retail. Let me explain.

WHOLESALE VERSUS RETAIL

Imagine you're going to buy a new truck. You pull into the parking lot of your local Chevrolet dealer. What happens? They've got five hundred vehicles on their lot, and you spend thirty minutes looking around. But then, suddenly, when you stop in front of one truck, the salesman who's been watching you comes out of nowhere to shake your hand. He shows you the price in the window of the truck. It is the "sticker price" of the vehicle.

Sticker = retail.

Hold that thought for a moment. Now, what are you going to do? You're a smart person. You're not going to pay sticker price for that truck, are you? No, you're going to go into the dealership, sit down at the cubicle with the salesperson, and likely go back and forth for the next thirty minutes trying to get them as close as possible to the "invoice price" of the truck.

Invoice = wholesale.

Think about it. If you asked the salesperson about price, they gave you the sticker price, and you said okay, do you think they would tell you the invoice price? No.

More to the point, **whether you pay sticker price or invoice price, retail or wholesale, you're going to be driving off the lot with the exact same truck.**

It's about educating yourself. Same thing when it comes to investing your hard-earned dollars. You know you can invest your money into mutual funds and pay lots of loads and fees up front, or you can use those exact funds with no loads or fees.

The difference is retail versus wholesale.

But you have to educate yourself on the different investments out there today. Educate yourself on the investments you have right now. Know what you're paying in fees. Know how much risk you're taking.

Coming back to what we discussed earlier, you must also

know what you want your money to do at this phase of your life. If you're like most of our clients, what you want is capital preservation—to hold on to what you have with growth either for income now or income in the future.

What does growth mean for you today? Right now, at this phase of life, **your focus should be on making 5 to 8 percent on your money and not getting blown up when the market goes down.**

Pull out your mutual fund, brokerage statement, and 401(k) s and look at them. We've talked a lot already in this chapter about safety and risk. Most people who are invested in the market don't just have five or ten stocks in their portfolio. Most have their money sitting in mutual funds because they're more diversified. This means that you're invested in 250 to 500 companies as part of one mutual fund.

With mutual funds, there's not as much risk because you're not putting all your eggs in one basket. Say you have 500 companies that make up one mutual fund and ten of those companies have a bad day—you're still probably going to end up with a good return. Not a lot of risk there.

So, what's the problem? The fees. According to *US News & World Report*, "including all of the hidden fees associated with mutual funds, the total cost of ownership is estimated to be over 4 percent annually for a taxable account."

KNOW YOUR FEES

A client came to us with $1.2 million and thought he was in control of how he was investing his money. With the previous firm he was working with, he would tell them how he wanted to invest and they would do it. But as he went through our process, we learned that out of his $1.2 million, he had about $550,000 in variable annuities and was paying at least 3 percent in fees, which added up to $16,500 each year.

Then he had another $350,000 in a mutual fund that was paying over 2 percent a year in fees. Finally, there was $150,000 in bonds at 1.25 percent a year in fees. Altogether, these combined fees added up to over $25,000 a year.

Not only that, but when we put his portfolio through a stress test, we found that if the market took a big hit, he could possibly lose $440,000.

All in all, this client had come to us thinking he was protected and in control, and assuming he was paying low fees. Turns out he had a downside of over 40 percent if the market crashed and was paying over $25,000 a year in fees!

In short, he was investing in the retail world, but thinking he was getting wholesale prices, all because of what his other advisor was not disclosing.

> Are you assuming you're paying low fees but don't really know?

If you want the wholesale price, you need to educate yourself on the fees you are paying. This is all the more important as you get closer to retirement, when you're nearing that preservation phase.

This is where you want to **plan for the worst and hope for the best**. A lot of people are only doing the second part of that equation. When they put money into a mutual fund or a variable annuity or stock, I'm sure they are hoping for the best, but chances are they're not really planning for the worst.

CHAPTER 4

ARE YOU ON THE RIGHT TRACK?

"It's not whether you get knocked down, it's whether you get up."

—VINCE LOMBARDI

When we meet with prospective clients, many of them ask us, "What exactly do you mean by 'plan for the worst and hope for the best'? What percentage of our hard-earned dollars should we have in the stock market? How much of our liquid assets, investible assets, should be in the market (at risk) versus being safe and sound somewhere else?"

The rule of thumb we use is called the **Rule of 100**, originated by John Bogle in the mid-seventies. John (or Jack, as he was known) is the founder of the Vanguard Group. I've had him on our radio show a couple times. Very humble individual. In fact, the reason he started Vanguard in the first place is that he was working for a big wire house when he came up with a great idea called index investing. Instead of embracing his idea, his employer fired him. Then, all of the big wire houses blackballed him and he couldn't find a job anywhere else. Why not? Because he was teaching us normal investors how to save a lot of money!

Bogle also came up with this rule where you take one hundred minus your age—so if you're sixty-five years old, you subtract that number from one hundred, which gives you thirty-five. The sixty-five number (your age) is also how much of your money, percentage-wise, you should have secure so that if the market experiences a 10 to 30 percent correction, it won't matter, because your money is more secure.

The other 35 percent should, of course, be in riskier investments where the money can grow because it's there for the long-term. In this case, 65/35 would be what we call the **safe/risk ratio**.

The Rule of 100 is a great place to start, but it's not right for everyone. This isn't a cookie-cutter approach. It's not a cure-all or fix-everything. Just because you're sixty-five, it doesn't mean your safe/risk ratio has to be 65/35. You must also take into consideration variables that are unique to you, such as your risk tolerance, income needs, lifestyle goals, family dynamics, liabilities, and assets.

> What percentage of *your* hard-earned dollars should you have in the (risky) stock market—the Wall Street world—and what percentage should you have somewhere safe?

THE THREE WORLDS

You want to make sure you are diversified throughout the three worlds of money. What I mean by this is, in my opinion, you have to have **a little bit of money in all three worlds: the banking world, the insurance world, and the Wall Street world.**

If you want money to be liquid and safe from market risk, you can put it in the *banking world*—specifically a bank, savings and loan, or credit union in a money market, savings, or a short-term CD.

If you want money to grow over the long term and keep up with the cost of living and inflation, you must be willing to take some risk to get the potential reward of higher returns. The *insurance world* offers principal protection and income you can never outlive, and allows you to protect your assets and your family while setting aside money to leave a legacy.

But if your advisor only works in one world, the *Wall Street world*, they simply don't have the necessary tools in their toolbox to help you in the way you need.

We use a doctor analogy. If you have a serious medical problem, you'll be sent to a specialist who knows how to treat that problem. And when it comes to retirement, a lot of people are working with a general practitioner, when what they really need is a retirement specialist.

> If your advisor only works in one world, the Wall Street world, he or she is going to want to put all of your money in the market—which, for retirement purposes, would be a mistake.

Look at your current situation. What are you invested in inside of your 401(k) or other qualified accounts? You need to look at your retirement funds in two different buckets: what you've already made and what you could make. In other words, if you have $500,000, $1,000,000, or $2,000,000 sitting in a 401(k), that's money you've made. But the mistake we commonly see today is that people are still investing that $500,000, $1,000,000, or $2,000,000 they've already made in the same way they're investing the new money that goes in every pay period. They're taking the same amount of risk.

As you get closer to retirement, you want to make sure you're *not* doing that. You want to be more conservative with that money you've already made that's in one bucket of your 401(k)—and then take more risk with the *new* money that's going in every pay period.

When the newly earned money is going into your 401(k) and the market is dropping, it's actually not a bad thing. With each pay period, you're buying into the market, and you're buying into it when it's down, which means you're going to have a bigger gain when it comes up.

Another important piece of advice here is that if you have 401(k)s and company plans, you need to make sure you're maxing those out. You should try to put away 15 to 20 percent of your income every year. Most companies that offer 401(k) plans or other retirement accounts have a certain maximum contribution that they will *match*. Definitely make sure you're putting in at least that much. After all, that's free money your employer is giving to you. It would be silly not to take advantage of it.

Always make sure to max out your company retirement plan!

UNDERSTAND YOUR FEES

Get to know your 401(k) and other retirement accounts through and through. What are the fees being charged by the administrators? What are the fees of the different subaccounts inside the 401(k) that you're invested in? If you have an advisor, what fees are *they* charging you? A lot of people get this piece wrong. They say their advisor is charging one fee. But then that advisor takes their money and throws it into mutual funds, where they're charged another fee. So they actually end up paying twice what they thought they were.

Then, there are also "variable annuities," which carry different fees. Per Investopedia, the different fees are:

- **Mortality and expense:** A fancy name for a life insurance fee—this fee compensates the issuer any losses that it might suffer for unexpected events, such as death. You are paying a fee to guarantee your beneficiaries receive at least the amount you put in.
- **Subaccounts:** Inside of a VA, you are invested in mutual funds, and mutual funds have costs that come along with them.
- **GMWB/GMIB:** Guaranteed minimum withdraw benefit / guaranteed minimum income benefit is an optional rider that can be applied to give you a guaranteed income every year.
- **GMDB:** With the guaranteed minimum death benefit, the insurance company is charging you a fee to have your death benefit grow at a certain percentage every year and lock in on each anniversary date.

These could add even more fees each year, and most people have no idea they're paying these fees—at least not until we stress-test their portfolio and break it down for them.

Often we learn that our clients haven't looked at the prospectus for their plan. We encourage you to educate yourself and check your prospectus: all of the fees are in there. Don't be afraid to ask your advisor exactly what fees you are being charged. And why shouldn't you? Whose money is it—yours or theirs?

When it comes to mutual funds, there are three main fees: loads, fund expenses, and turnover ratio.

LOAD FEES

According to Investopedia, "Sales charges or commissions are known as 'the load' of a mutual fund. When a mutual fund has a front-end load, fees are assessed when shares are purchased. For a back-end load, mutual fund fees are assessed when an investor sells his shares. Sometimes, however, an investment company offers a no-load mutual fund, which doesn't carry any commission or sales charge."

If you look at your mutual fund, it will probably have an A, B, or C behind it. If you have an A behind your mutual fund, it means you are charged the load up front before your money ever goes to work. They take the load right off the top. If the average load share is 5.75 percent, they will take that percentage off the top. Every time you add money to the account, they also take the load off the top. So, basically, you're losing 6 percent before your money ever goes to work for you. That's called an up-front load.

Now, if you don't have an A behind your mutual fund, you may have a B or C—in which case you're not being charged an up-front load. But if you draw that money out in the first six to eight years, you're charged the load on the backside. This is known as a back-end load.

With these mutual funds with an A, B, or C behind them, you get the same mutual fund with what's called a class F share. Class F means that you pay no load to get in or out. If you have an A share, you just pay sticker price for that mutual fund.

FUND EXPENSES

Fund expenses are just what they sounds like—the fees that mutual fund companies charge you to manage your money. According to Morningstar, an independent third party that rates mutual funds, fund expenses average 1.36 percent every year, whether you make money or not.

> Mutual funds charge annual fees (called expense ratios) that can eat into rates of return, reducing the fund's overall payout.

TURNOVER RATIO

If you have a mutual fund made up of 250 stocks, for example, turnover ratio refers to the number of times in a year that the mutual fund manager is taking those 250 stocks, selling them, and buying all new ones. In other words, they are *turning over* your portfolio.

According to Investopedia, the turnover ratio or turnover rate is defined as "the percentage of a mutual fund or other portfolio's holdings that have been replaced in a given year."

Anytime you buy or sell a stock, what do you have? You have trading desk costs, and guess who those trading desk costs are passed on to? The people who own shares of those mutual funds.

An average trading desk cost is 1.44 percent. When you take 1.3 percent in fund expenses, plus 1.4 percent average trading desk cost, you're charged 2.7 percent every single year, whether you make or lose money.

Again, that's retail versus wholesale.

It's why it's so important to understand the investments you have and exactly what you want your money to do for you.

CHAPTER 5

TAKING CONTROL OF YOUR RETIREMENT

There are two kinds of retirement monies: nonqualified and qualified.

Nonqualified money is the money you have already paid taxes on, money you have in your checking and savings accounts.

Qualified money is money you've never paid taxes on—money that's *qualified* to be taxed.

Most of you have qualified accounts. These are your 401(k)s, 403(b)s, or TSA accounts. If you work for the federal government, you may have what's called a TSP, a Thrift Savings Plan. If you are retired, you may have already taken your 401(k) and rolled over into an IRA. If you're self-employed, you may have a simple IRA. All of these are qualified accounts you have never paid taxes on.

401(K) PLANS VERSUS PENSIONS

Up until 1978, the only retirement plan available was a defined benefit plan, also known as a pension. A little was taken out of your paycheck each pay period and put into a plan that the company would hold and earn interest on. When you retired, you received a monthly income stream. But that income stream ended when you and your spouse passed away. Nothing went to your beneficiaries even though you might have contributed for a long time.

In 1978, 401(k) plans started, and they are what most people have now. A 401(k) is defined as a "company sponsored retirement account that employees can contribute to," and "employers may also make matching contributions" (Investopedia). When an employee retires, it is their money, to do with what they want. The problem lies in the fact that if you don't invest it properly, it may not last throughout your lifetime. You could run out of money.

According to Investopedia, "In recent decades, 401(k) plans have become more plentiful and traditional pensions increasingly rare, as employers have shifted the responsibility and risk of saving for retirement to their employees."

THE SECURE ACT

The SECURE Act is a new law that went into effect January 1, 2020. SECURE stands for Setting Every Community Up for Retirement Enhancement. It is important to understand what it means for you.

First, it limits "stretch IRAs," meaning that instead of withdrawals from an inherited (non-spouse) IRA being stretched over the lifetime of the beneficiary, many beneficiaries will be required to take withdrawals within ten years after the original account owner has passed.

Stretch IRAs are basically gone. So, what's the wisest move for you? How can you structure your multigenerational IRA (MGIRA) strategy to create a legacy of lifetime income for your spouse, children, and grandchildren? Developing a strategy using life insurance and/or Roth IRAs is a great way to make sure your money is passed on to your beneficiaries and not the IRS.

Second, there is no age limit anymore for contributing to IRAs like 401(k)s and Roth IRAs. This means that if you're older than 70.5 and still working, you can keep making contributions.

Third, in terms of required minimum distributions (RMDs), if you were not 70.5 by the end of 2019, you can now wait until age 72 to begin taking RMDs.

With these RMD dates changing, what should *you* do with yours? If you don't need income immediately, don't take your RMD at 70.5. Wait until you are 72 so your money can stay in a tax-deferred account a little longer.

Fourth, there is now something called an annual disclosure of lifetime income from defined contribution plans. This means that plans are now required to show participants how much income could be generated from their current lump-sum balance.

There are a few other changes to note, such an annuity allocation in 401(k)s, smaller employer retirement plans, and penalty-free distributions.

As you can see, there are a lot of different options with the new SECURE Act, and you need to be sure you have a retirement specialist who is updating you on these types of changes.

PART THREE

———

BUILDING YOUR PLAN

I coached high-school football for ten years at a very high level. During that period, I always prided myself on the fact that our team was able to win against teams that were bigger, faster, and stronger than us. Why? Because our coaches and players prepared and practiced more than the other teams we faced.

This was especially true when our team reached the semifinals of the 7A Illinois High School Playoffs and were pitted against the best team in the Chicago Catholic League, St. Rita of Cascia High School. This team outweighed us at each position by at least fifty pounds!

They jumped out to a 14–0 lead in the first quarter, but we came back and ended up winning 21–14 on a score late in the game.

Everyone was surprised except our team and coaches. We knew we had the discipline and could pull off a win if we stuck to our game plan. St. Rita had over 130 yards in penalties, compared to our fifteen yards in penalties.

We did not waver from our disciplined game plan, which is what we preach to our clients all the time.

Just like the four quarters of a football game, there are going to be a lot of ups and downs. But you must stay disciplined, trust your team, be proactive, and remain confident in the plan you have built.

CHAPTER 6

WHAT DO YOU HAVE IN YOUR BUCKETS?

"Hope for the best, plan for the worst."

—LEE CHILD

Recently, we met with some clients who thought they had a solid game plan for their continued retirement. They started with a nice nest egg. Now that they were retired, they needed this money to live on. Nine months later, however, they had lost over 40 percent because the majority of their portfolio was invested in the market.

As we often explain to our clients, financial planning doesn't have to be difficult, but you do need to put in the work to look at your money critically.

DON'T LOOK FOR THE EASY WAY OUT

When I was in fourth grade, we had to take standardized state tests at the end of the school year to make sure our education was on track and we could move up to the next grade. I was never the smartest kid in the room. I was a solid B, maybe C, student and usually the last person done with tests. I just wasn't a strong test-taker.

Then, one day while on the school bus heading home, an older kid who I looked up to told me his secret tip for answering multiple-choice questions. He said, "If you don't know the answer, always put C. It will be right most of the time."

The following week was our state testing, and I was ready to go. The teacher had asked us to bring something to keep us occupied in case we finished our tests before the rest of the class. I showed up with two books to read because I knew that, with my new secret test-taking weapon, I was going to have a lot of free time over the next four days of testing.

Again, I may not have been the smartest kid in the room, but at that moment, I thought I was the cleverest. When the test started, I began filling in my answers slowly, but as soon as I noticed that the first kid in the room had finished his test, I marked the rest of the answers with C. I did the same thing for the next three days. It felt great finishing my tests early and I just knew the kids were thinking, "Wow, Chad is really, really smart."

You can probably guess where this is going. Fast-forward to the first day of fifth grade after summer vacation. A teacher came into my class and pulled me out. She then proceeded to walk me down to the special education room. My testing method had, shockingly to me, not worked. It had proven that I wasn't as smart as I thought.

That day, I went home and told my mom everything. Luckily for me, she then made a trip to the principal's office and got it all straightened out. I got in some trouble over the whole thing, but I learned a lesson from it.

Don't look for the easy way out. In order to have the payoff of a successful retirement, you have to put in the work. Oftentimes, people procrastinate planning for retirement. They don't have the time to put a plan together.

What they don't realize is that there isn't an easy way out. You can't rely on the government or your employer any longer. You can't wait until you start losing money or until your plan starts failing before you start preparing for retirement. By then it will be too late.

Hard work beats talent when talent doesn't work hard.

Again, financial planning doesn't have to be difficult, but you have to be smart and strategic about it, especially about separating your money into **three different buckets: the secure bucket, growth bucket, and dream bucket.**

THE THREE BUCKETS

The money in the **secure bucket** is just like it says: secure. If the market has a 10 to 20 percent correction, you cannot afford to lose that money. You want to make sure that the funds in the secure bucket are protected from downturns in the market, so they are able to give you that income stream you need for the rest of your life and your spouse's life, no matter how long either of you lives.

Once your secure bucket is set up and you have an income stream that you know will always be there, *then* you can put some other money in the **growth bucket**, where it can grow. It's there to keep up with the rate of inflation and cost of living. If the market's down, it's not a big deal. Why? Because you don't have to lock any of those losses; you have a plan in place with that secure bucket. When the market's up, you can harvest some of those gains.

Once you have a secure bucket and a growth bucket, you can start a **dream bucket.** The point of the dream bucket is to set aside something for yourself and those you love so that you can enjoy life. Maybe you have money set aside for a second home in the mountains or at the lake. Maybe you want to take your kids and grandkids on one big trip every year, or maybe your dream is that your kids never have to worry if something happens to you or if you need to be taken care of in your old age, which could mean long-term care, home healthcare, or assisted-living facilities.

To be clear, not everyone finds the dream bucket necessary. Some people only want to split their money into the secure bucket and the growth bucket, and that is fine.

We had a couple, Jerry and Theresa, who attended our Empower University courses. They were blue-collar workers who had been working hard for over forty years and wanted to know if they could retire. Their biggest concern had to do with Jerry's age. He was sixty-two years old and worked as a sheet-metal worker for a heating and cooling company. He worked with his hands and had to climb on buildings and do a lot of tough blue-collar work. His body was worn out. When they would come in to meet with me, Theresa would express how concerned she was that Jerry would have to do this backbreaking labor for the rest of their lives just to provide income for them to live on, because they did not have a retirement game plan—and she didn't know where else their income could come from.

So we sat down with them and built a plan for the money they had. We figured out that with the pension Jerry was going to receive, the income from his 401(k), and the new investment strategy we set up for him, he could indeed retire now if he wanted.

Within a month of our setting up the plan for him, that's exactly what he did! His wife cried tears of joy.

> "Life isn't about waiting for the storm to pass; it's about learning to dance in the rain. It's about removing the fear in this area of your life so you can focus on what matters most."
>
> —TONY ROBBINS

ANALYZING YOUR SAFE/RISK RATIO

When a couple came to us—we'll call them Fred and Linda—he was an electrical lineman and she was a retired schoolteacher. They had a very healthy nest egg of $1.5 million but were rightfully concerned about market volatility. Their money went up and down; their accounts had no stability. They had already been working with a growth specialist, but they came to us because they smartly realized that, at their age, they needed to now be working with a retirement specialist.

We looked at their portfolio and split their money into the three buckets: the secure bucket, the growth bucket, and the dream bucket. Fred and Linda had plenty of money to live off of for normal living expenses, but in their case, they had a bucket list of things they wanted to accomplish, and on that list was visiting every continent. Traveling was something they loved to do together. Knowing this, we were able to give them the income they needed but also build a game plan for providing that extra money every year to travel.

The biggest issue we see with the safe/risk ratio is that **people don't know how much risk they are taking until after they have an analysis done,** like what we do with our clients. We show people like Fred and Linda exactly how much risk they have, so if the market were to experience a 10 to 20 percent correction, they would be prepared and know how much money they stand to lose.

Thankfully for Fred and Linda, there were no terrible consequences. They found the specialists they needed—us—in time to make the necessary diagnoses and prescriptions. I am happy to report that they are now indeed traveling the world and living their dreams.

But often it's too late. Many people have no idea of the reality until we show them their risk and also the fees that are eating up their gains.

Unless you have the right kind of advisor, you don't know what you don't know. And because this couple's previous advisors came from a growth perspective rather than a retirement perspective—because they only worked in one world—they were at risk.

CHAPTER 7

WHAT ARE THE VEHICLES YOU CAN USE?

"Even if you are on the right track, you'll get run over if you just sit there."

—WILL ROGERS

I want to be clear that, in my opinion, there is no such thing as a bad investment vehicle. However, **certain vehicles are set up for certain people in certain phases of their life.** Variable annuities are set up for younger people who are willing to take some risk and who need tax advantages and a death benefit. For retirees, however, it's a completely different story. I have found that variable annuities are one of the worst investment vehicles for retirees. They go up and down with the market, and a lot of excess fees are involved in those accounts.

We had another married couple who attended our workshop a couple of years ago, but in their case, they had already been retired for six years. The gentleman had retired from AT&T at age fifty-nine with $1.4 million in a 401(k) that they rolled over to an IRA. The wife had a small pension coming in, and they had thought that when they turned sixty-two, their Social Security would kick in and they would be able to live comfortably for the rest of their lives. Now, they were coming to us at age sixty-five for a complimentary consultation.

Anytime somebody comes in to meet with me, I ask them what kind of questions or concerns they have. This couple came to me concerned because they had worked with three different advisors over the previous six years. The advisors had told them that they had to have a majority of their money in the market for the long term so it would last as long as they do.

They needed to draw $25,000 a year off of that $1.4 million to live off of. If you do the math, this means they had to have less than a 2 percent return on this money to get them the $25,000 a year they needed. But when I sat down with them after they'd been retired for six years, I learned that their $1.4 million was now down to under $690,000.

You read that right: they'd lost over half of their assets! How did this happen? There were three issues at play here. The first problem had to do with how the money had been invested and left vulnerable to market volatility. Second, they'd been drawing the money out. Third, much of their money had been invested in a variable annuity.

We were able to take the remaining $690,000, build a proper safe/risk ratio, and protect the rest of what they had.

But they, and many others, often tell us they wish they had met us ten years ago.

What we would have done for them is find the right, appropriate vehicles in the banking and insurance world for their secure bucket, in the Wall Street world for their growth bucket, and in the Wall Street and insurance world for their dream bucket.

Let's tackle these one by one.

VEHICLES IN THE SECURE BUCKET

First, we'll look at investment vehicles for the secure bucket, which is the bucket where you want to keep a certain portion of your money safe and liquid in case you need to access it. The money in the secure bucket avoids large swings in value. Vehicles sitting in this bucket can include your checking account, savings account, CDs, money market accounts, and fixed annuities.

The secure bucket is the foundation of your retirement strategy.

Why is it so important to have a foundation? We ask everyone in our workshops, "What's the most used part of your house?" Some say their kitchen, others their living room, man cave, and so on. Then I tell them, "Actually the most important part of your house is the foundation." If you have 60 or 70 percent of your house in your living room, kitchen, or bedroom, and a big financial storm comes along, it's going to blow your whole house over. But if you have a solid foundation—where 60 to 70 percent of your portfolio is in good, secure investments—for the most part, your house will be protected.

As long as the product terms are followed, you will not lose this money, but people often don't like to talk about this bucket because it's boring. It's not sexy.

The main things to address here are annuities and life insurance. Two types of annuities fit in the secure bucket: immediate and fixed.

With immediate, you put your money in the annuity and begin drawing an income stream right away to last you the rest of your life. But you also have to remember that whenever you decide to turn on this income stream, it will lock in whatever the interest rates are at the time. So if interest rates are not very strong currently, you may not get much more back over time beyond your principal.

Fixed annuities, on the other hand, are different, in that you cannot lose your principal. Any time you make a gain or lock in a gain, it becomes your new principal. There are three types of fixed annuities:

1. The MYGA is a multi-year guaranteed annuity. When you put your money in it, you get a set rate for a period of time. When that time is over, you can take your money and do whatever you want with it.

2. The fixed-index annuity tracks an index. If you have an index like the S&P 500, you put your money in there, but you're not actually investing in the index. It just tracks what the index does over a period of time, for example, every month or year. If there is a gain in that index, you don't get to keep all of the gain, but you do get a portion of it and you lock it in. It becomes your new principal.

3. The third kind is the fixed annuity with an income rider. You can get an income rider anywhere from 5 to 7 percent that will securely let your money grow at a certain rate each year. Whatever age you decide to turn that on, it will determine the payout you will receive for the

rest of your life. It gives you an income stream that you will never outlive.

There are three main reasons to use annuities in your portfolios: first, preservation of principal, meaning protecting the money you have available to invest (protecting your nest egg); second, to give you an income that you can never outlive; and third, wealth transfer.

If you put your money in the stock market, you have no idea what's going to happen.

Your goal should be to have enough money sitting in your secure bucket to give you and your spouse an income stream coming in every month for the rest of your lives to support your lifestyle.

As we have learned throughout this book, pensions are dying out—so you have to be proactive and build your own game plan. Annuities are becoming more and more mainstream. Twenty years ago, "annuities" was a bad word. But now even the government recognizes that people need annuities inside of their 401(k)s because pensions are dying out.

Think about your secure bucket as a way to **take some of your own savings and retirement accounts and build your own private pension plan or your family pension plan.**

VEHICLES IN THE GROWTH BUCKET

Once your secure bucket is set up, you can add the growth bucket. Money in the growth bucket is there to grow and to keep up with the rate of inflation, the cost of living. Your growth bucket can include mutual funds, real estate, index funds, options, stocks, or ETFs. **The money in the growth bucket is higher risk but also a lot higher reward**, and more exciting and sexier. When it grows, you make money. But on the flip side, it can be stressful in down times when it's not growing.

This is why it's so important to invest in the *right* companies—good, solid US companies. If the market goes down, these companies will suffer a small hit, but they are likely to come back and pay a good dividend.

There are many good, solid dividend-paying companies that we recommend our clients use, no matter what happens in the market. They pay anywhere from a 4 to 6 percent dividend each and every year. If you put $100,000 into a good, solid company's stock and it pays a 6 percent dividend, and that stock doesn't grow at all, it will still be worth $100,000 and will pay you $6,000 a year in income in the form of a dividend.

Most of our clients will take that dividend and buy more shares of that stock so their money is constantly compounded. But let's say that you need to draw some income from that growth bucket and the market is down. If your money is sitting in mutual funds that don't pay a dividend, you will have to sell shares of those mutual funds at a loss to get the income you need, which will magnify your losses.

But if you have stocks that pay dividends and you need income, all you need to do is, instead of reinvesting those dividends, take that 5 to 6 percent and put it in your pocket. You're not selling those shares of stock or locking in any losses. You are just taking the profits off of those stocks.

If you want to be more diversified in your account, instead of investing in open-end mutual funds, invest in index funds. These are basically funds that track the S&P 500 index. The idea is that we pay money managers anywhere from 1 to 3 percent a year to try to beat the index, the S&P, or the Dow Jones, just to name a few, but what we find is that, on average, the majority of the time, these money managers cannot outperform the index they're tracking.

Index funds are a solid alternative. They're a lot more cost-efficient and lower in fees but also more passive. They're not trying to beat the market but just track the market.

Bonds are another option for your growth bucket. A corporate bond, as defined by Investopedia, is an investment in debt that is issued by a company and sold by an investor. The company gets the cash it needs, and in return the investor is paid a pre-established number of interest payments. When the bond expires, or "reaches maturity," the payments cease and the original investment is returned.

When you buy corporate bonds, essentially you are loaning your money to the company. For instance, if you invest $100,000 in a bond with Coca-Cola, they will pay you a return every year on your original investment. But to get a good-quality bond today, you must be willing to put your money in there for a longer period of time. If you draw it out before the maturity date is up, you can lose some of that money.

With bonds, if interest rates go up, bond values go down. If, for example, you had a $100,000 bond with a twenty-year maturity and you drew it out in ten years, you might only get back $80,000. But if you can hold that bond to maturity, you will eventually get your original amount back.

With the growth bucket, it all depends on where you're at with regard to your age and risk tolerance. Mutual funds— meaning an investment vehicle that's made up of a pool of money including stocks, bonds, or other securities—are good when you're younger and trying to build wealth. But as you get older and have more wealth, you should look at individual stocks and index funds, which are portfolios of stocks or bonds designed to mimic the composition and performance of a financial market index.

You want to grow your money but protect yourself from unnecessary fees. At this stage it becomes more about capital preservation.

Again, there's no such thing as a bad investment vehicle. Mutual funds are very good when you're younger and trying to build wealth. They are higher risk but also higher reward. But the problem is that people continue to invest in the same vehicles after retirement. Investing in the same vehicles throughout your entire life and not evolving as you enter different phases can be detrimental to your retirement portfolio.

All in all, the vehicles we've covered here in the growth bucket section are higher risk but also higher reward. They can be exciting, especially when they're working, but stressful when they're not working.

VEHICLES IN THE DREAM BUCKET

In thinking about your dream bucket, you need to ask yourself: what are some extras that you want in retirement? Do you dream about a second home in the mountains or in Florida or Arizona? Do you want to invest in an RV or a boat? Do you want to take your kids and grandkids on an annual trip to the beach or skiing or to Disney? Remember, your dream bucket can be used for things you don't actually *need* but that excite you!

For some people, however, their dream retirement isn't anything extravagant. It's staying close to home, spending time with family, and watching their children and grandchildren grow. Often, people who choose to live a low-key retirement have a lump sum of money that they would like to pass on to their beneficiaries.

Some clients have a lump sum from their IRAs or qualified accounts. This is money they do not need to live off of—but if they live long enough, at age seventy-two, the government is going to make them draw out their RMDs. When they draw out that money, they can build another pile of money to be left to their beneficiaries tax-free. The way to do that is **with life insurance.**

It may sound strange, but life insurance is used in many different ways these days. Think about it like this: twenty years ago, what did we use our phone for? Just to call people. But now we use it for a calendar, a camera, the internet, and so much more. Life insurance is similar, in that twenty years ago, it was strictly for the purpose of taking care of your debt if you passed away. Now, however, it is used for all sorts of things, including a max death benefit for your beneficiaries and long-term care protection for you.

> Life insurance is a great way to build a tax-free inheritance for your beneficiaries and/or to plan for your own long-term care.

PART FOUR

———

STAYING ON TRACK

Staying on track is about resilience. It's not enough to just implement your proactive retirement plan; you have to *stick to it.*

The ability to stay on track doesn't come easy to everyone. It is a skill that I learned over time, through many years of setting goals—some of them I reached; others I didn't.

As we get ready to send our oldest child off to college, I find myself reminiscing quite a bit. If I were to point to one skill or life experience that has prepared my oldest son for this life ahead, I would have to say it's *failure.* Learning how to accept failure, take responsibility for failure, and persevere after failure—these are the keys to staying on track with your life goals, whatever they may be.

I spent four years in college studying sociology and knowing that I was born to be a police officer. It was all I wanted to do. I took the tests, I trained, but in the end, I never got that phone call. So I went back to my summer job doing concrete work and resigned myself to the fact that this might be the rest of my life—even *with* a college education.

Then one day, I answered an ad in the paper for a job. All it said was that the employer was looking for a sports-minded, competitive person. The job turned out to be a sales position, going door-to-door selling Medicare Supplement and long-term care insurance. I never really pictured myself in a role like this, but I spoke with my parents and they said this was "okay to do until you find a real job."

To be honest, I just wanted to get out of concrete work.

And now, here I am, twenty-six years, seven offices, and four kids later—and there's no concrete mix in sight. I'd say it worked out.

Through it all, I had failures but also successes. Both brought me to the place where I am now, but especially the failures. In our house, we celebrate not only when our kids have straight As but also when they work hard to pull up their grades from a C to an A. We celebrate our children when they *don't* make a team but decide to put in more effort and work on their skills so that they can try out again next year. We celebrate when they show up every day to practice, knowing they may not get in the game. We celebrate when they overcome the adversity of having a teacher who they don't see eye-to-eye with—because we know they may someday have a boss like that.

All in all, I'm proud to say that we celebrate our failures as much as we do the successes that follow.

Having raised our kids this way, I now have the peace of mind in knowing that our children will never quit. They may not be in the top of their class. They may not get scholarships for athleticism. But they will be humble, and they will never give up.

The saying in our home is "If you're not growing, you're dying." Goal-setting is imperative in your personal and professional lives. Lots of people give lip service to setting goals. They set them all the time but eventually break the promises they've made to themselves. Other people require an army of people to believe in them before they can finally achieve their goals.

In my view, there is only one person you need to believe in—and that's yourself.

CHAPTER 8

WHAT ARE YOU DOING TO STAY ACCOUNTABLE?

"Ninety-nine percent of the failures come from people who have the habit of making excuses."

—GEORGE WASHINGTON CARVER

Things happen in life that you didn't plan for. It's vitally important to build a budget and to stick to that budget. Don't spend more than what your budget originally called for. If you do, then those are adjustments you need to make in your portfolio.

We see a lot of people who end up having to change their budget because their grown children need their financial help. That, of course, is their choice. Me, I'm old school. I believe you are responsible for getting your kids to and through college. But after that, they should pretty much be on their own. **You should not dwindle your life savings or retirement accounts to take care of your kids.**

LIFE HAPPENS

We talk about a dream bucket, but because these unexpected things come along in life, you need to have an advisor who is with you every step of the way to update your plan if needed.

Like I mentioned at the beginning of the book, my grandparents were my inspiration for getting into this business. Life happened, and they were not prepared for the unexpected. They didn't have a plan, and my grandmother had to work basically work until she died.

Because of what I learned from her experience, I bought life insurance and long-term care for my parents.

You have to plan when it comes to long-term care. In my opinion, there are three options available. The first is to pay for it out of your own pocket. It's usually around $6,000 to $10,000 a month, and that is increasing all the time (the numbers could be double fifteen or twenty years from now). Clearly, this can add up very quickly and wipe out the nest egg that you've spent thirty to forty years accumulating.

The second option is to buy a long-term care insurance policy. But what happens if you pay into that policy for twenty years and never need it? You'll be out all of the money you put in each year, with nothing to show for it. Not only that, but premiums from the insurance carriers increase about every five years, which means you're likely going to be paying significantly higher premiums twenty years into your policy than you did the first couple years.

The third and final option when it comes to planning for long-term care is the most sensible and effective: pay into a life insurance policy that offers long-term care benefits. Many life insurance policies offer some type of long-term care rider, and some even offer a benefit that is built into the policy.

For example, say that you and your wife are both in your seventies, in good health, and getting ready to start drawing required minimum distributions (RMDs) from your qualified accounts. You do not need this money to live off of, but would like to add some long-term care protection, as well as a legacy to your children, or grandchildren if you were to pass away.

You decide to each pay $10,000 a year into a life insurance policy. Based on your age and health, you will each have a life insurance policy that gives you around $300,000 to $350,000 in death benefits. If one of you were to pass away, that money would be passed on to your beneficiaries tax-free.

The tax-free legacy that life insurance leaves to your loved ones is one of its biggest benefits.

Another benefit is the long-term care addition. Let's say you get very ill and cannot perform at least two of the six activities of daily living: eating, bathing, dressing, toileting, transferring, maintaining continence. With this new life insurance policy, you'll be able to access a portion of the death benefit for long-term care purposes.

Typically, each company allows around 24 percent annually, or 2 percent monthly, from the death benefit. In this case, you would be able to access approximately $84,000 (or $7,000 monthly) in the first year for long-term care purposes. This means you could use these benefits for about four years before the death benefit is depleted.

As you can see, this is a great option for those looking for long-term care benefits. Not only do you have access to the death benefit for long-term care purposes, but if you never need them, they will be passed on to your loved ones in the form of a tax-free death benefit.

Unlike traditional long-term care insurance, you are not out all that money if you end up not needing the funds for long-term care purposes. For all of these reasons, we believe this is a very beneficial option, and much more advantageous than paying out of pocket or buying a long-term care insurance policy.

TAKING CARE OF YOUR SPOUSE

If you retire with a pension, you have the option of taking 100 percent for yourself, which is called a single life payout, or a joint and survivor payout. Joint and survivor pensions make a single monthly payment but, as opposed to single life, have *two* beneficiaries. Joint and survivor pensions pay a monthly income until both beneficiaries pass away. Because they will likely have to pay benefits for longer than a single life pension, joint and survivor pensions usually pay less than a single life. This means you are giving up some of your monthly income in exchange for the peace of mind that your spouse will continue to receive that income even after you're gone. That is something to discuss with your spouse and plan for. If something happens to you, how will your spouse pay the bills to meet the budget to continue to live her lifestyle? I say "her" because normally women outlive men. Have you planned for that?

Bob, a seventy-year-old client of mine, had already made the decision to take the full pension when he came in to see me. He was watching our TV show when he started questioning this decision. He realized that even though the single life payout option would pay a higher monthly amount than a joint survivor payout option, it would stop paying once the recipient dies.

This client was doing great living off Social Security and getting $4,000 a month. But once you set up a pension, it's irrevocable. Bob's biggest concern was that if he passed away, his wife would get nothing. If that happened, she would probably have to sell the house and completely change her lifestyle.

Nobody wants to think about going to a nursing home or dying; nobody wants to think about a time when his or her better half may not be around anymore. But you have to be proactive about these things and plan ahead for them so there will be no surprises. You will do your family a huge disservice if you don't plan properly.

CHAPTER 9

WHAT IS YOUR PLAN GOING FORWARD?

"Whatever you want to do, do it now. There are only so many tomorrows."

—MICHAEL LANDON

We hear it all the time from our clients: "We've worked thirty to forty years to get to retirement. We don't want to have to manage our money once we retire." It's understandable. People want to enjoy their retirement, play golf, spend time with their kids and grandkids, and travel.

Or sometimes clients say, "We don't want to manage our own money, but we want to *know what's going on* with our money." They're right. You shouldn't have to manage your own money. Your advisor is there to guide, educate, and empower you to make better decisions with your hard-earned dollars. But they're *not* there to dictate what you should actually do with your money.

This is why it's so important to educate yourself. Find out where your money is invested and how these vehicles work. Know the proper questions to ask and make your own decisions.

The journey of a thousand miles begins with the first step. For many of our clients, the first step is watching our TV show, coming to one of our workshops, or setting an appointment to meet for a complimentary consultation.

As far as questions to ask yourself, there are a few things that you should be able to answer or that your financial advisor should be open to helping you figure out:

How much are you paying in fees?

How much risk are you taking?

How long will your money last?

FIDUCIARY VERSUS SUITABILITY STANDARD

The suitability standard means that an investment must meet the suitability requirements outlined in FINRA Rule

2111 prior to being recommended by a firm to an investor (Investopedia). If you have an advisor who works for a wire house or bank, they have to recommend investment vehicles that are "suitable" for you (because they clear through a broker-dealer). But that doesn't mean that they're necessarily recommending what's *best* for you.

> A broker-dealer is a person or firm in the business of buying and selling securities for its own account or on behalf of its customers (Investopedia).

If you have a *fiduciary*, however, that's a different story.

A fiduciary, as defined by Investopedia, is a person or organization that acts on behalf of another person or persons to manage assets. Essentially, a fiduciary owes to that other entity the duties of good faith and trust. The highest legal duty of one party to another, being a fiduciary requires being bound ethically to act in the other's best interests.

A fiduciary not only has to meet FINRA Rule 2111, suitability, but also has to do what is in the client's best interest, not what's in the company's best interest. In most parts of the world, financial professionals have a duty to take steps that ensure the investment is suitable for a client. For example, in the United States, the Financial Industry Regulatory Authority (FINRA) oversees and enforces these rules. Suitability standards are not the same as fiduciary requirements.

At Slagle Financial, we are a fiduciary and therefore must do what is in the client's best interest, not what's in the company's best interest. Furthermore, we work in all three worlds: banking, insurance, and Wall Street. Many advisors work in one industry: a broker who only works in Wall Street, an insurance agent who works only in the insurance world. Remember, you need an advisor who works in all three worlds.

If you already have an advisor, do you know what kind of advisor they are? A lot of clients who come to us from other places didn't know who they were dealing with before. They would just open up a brokerage statement and see that they had an advisor who said they were a fiduciary. Meanwhile, the client was sitting in only three or four mutual fund companies, when there are thousands of mutual fund companies out there.

If this sounds like you, you're probably dealing with an advisor who has to go by the suitability standard. You need to find out: are you working with a commission-based advisor or a fee-based advisor?

If you're working with a commission-based advisor and they take your money and put it into an A, B, or C share mutual fund, they will charge you a load up front or on the backside. If they charge you a load up front, they make all their money right away, before your money ever goes to work for you. That's what an advisor does when they're someone who goes by the suitability standard.

If you work with a fee-based advisor, on the other hand, it means that if you make money, they make money. If you lose money, they lose money. Let's say they charge you a 1.5 percent fee. That fee is then divided by four every quarter. So if your money is worth more than it was, that will work out to a bigger fee for them. But if your money goes down, they will get less. **A fee-based advisor is in this with you— they're going to do everything they can to manage your money and make sure it grows consistently year in and year out.**

One lady who attended our workshops called me the next day to tell me she had reached out to her advisor to ask what she was paying in fees, and he got mad at her for asking!

Again, whose money is it—yours or theirs? When you invest your hard-earned dollars, everything should be transparent.

MEET WITH YOUR ADVISOR OFTEN

You should be meeting with your advisor every three to six months, and the advisor should be using those meetings to bring you up to date with what's happening in the market and constantly making sure you are on track.

Many advisors work for wire houses or banks or broker-dealers; they're just order-takers. They call you occasionally and say they have a certain bond or investment they'd like to put your money in. That's not being a good guide. That's not financial planning. That's just somebody trying to sell you something. A good advisor should be up to speed with new laws and changes and how they affect your portfolio.

Similarly, many advisors will try to invest everyone in the same cookie-cutter accounts that they have previously had success with. A good advisor will build a plan *first* and then find the vehicles that fit your personalized plan.

Your guide should feel almost like a friend: someone who is with you every step of the way on this journey through retirement.

TOP TEN QUESTIONS TO ASK POTENTIAL ADVISORS

1. Are you a true fiduciary?
2. How do you get paid?
3. What extra fees should I be aware of?
4. What are your qualifications?
5. What is your investment philosophy?
6. Who is your custodian?
7. Do you have a set account minimum?
8. How often do you communicate with your clients?
9. What services does your firm provide?
10. What makes your client experience unique?

You should feel like you have the best coach in the world. Everyone needs that. Even the best athletes in the world. A great example of this was Tiger Woods in the 2019 Masters. I think everyone can agree that Tiger Woods is one of the best golfers of all time. He has dedicated his life to the sport and puts hard work in day in, day out. However, that Sunday in Augusta, Woods was falling behind. Joe LaCava, his caddie, pulled him aside and gave him a pep talk. Tiger Woods finished that day as the 2019 Masters champion, and he credited that talk with LaCava as the turning point of his big comeback.

A good coach is the difference between good and great. A good athlete may win a few championships. But not fifteen, like Tiger Woods. Not unless they have a coach to make them better.

You have put in hard work for thirty to forty years. Working day in, day out and putting money away for retirement. Sure, if you wanted to spend a few hours every day managing your portfolio in retirement, you could probably build a good financial plan and be somewhat successful.

When it comes to your money, it's hard to not let emotions get involved. No matter how good you are at managing your money. When the market goes volatile, it's hard to not get that "stinkin' thinkin'"—that is, a bad way of thinking that makes you believe you will fail and bad things are bound to happen to you.

That's another reason to have a coach to keep you on track, to give you that pep talk when the going gets tough and the market looks rough.

When it comes down to it, most clients don't want to put hours a day into managing their portfolio. They want to enjoy life, not worry about life.

Retirement planning is not about the destination; it's about the journey. Financial planning today doesn't have to be complicated, but you do have to be disciplined. Yes, you should have an advisor so you don't have to worry about it.

But equally important when it comes to an advisor is that you have someone holding you accountable, making sure you stick to the plan, and working every day to make sure your retirement finances stay on track.

WHAT MAKES US DIFFERENT?

When a prospective client sits down with an advisor, the advisor usually tells them that they will do three things: provide great customer service, build a customized financial plan, and manage all of the client's money. If the advisor tells the client they will do all of these things single-handedly, they will be average, if not poor, at each one.

A good advisor should have an experienced team at their back to help them be great at everything they promise clients. Next, they need to do a good job of building the financial plan for the client, and they need to stay in front of the client, scheduling reviews, in order to change the plan as life changes because, as we've seen, life does happen.

At Slagle Financial, when it comes to managing your money, we work with CFPs, CFAs, and money managers whose job it is to sit at a computer every day and monitor these accounts. This is what sets us apart from other advisors. We have experts who actively watch your money every day and make sure it is performing as it should for your personalized game plan. We don't just throw your money into a bunch of mutual funds.

When we talk about staying accountable and going forward, too many advisors today try to be all things to all people. In one day's time, the average advisor will sit down with a twenty-year-old, a thirty-year-old, and a forty-year-old, and then suddenly a sixty-five-year-old who is ready to retire walks through that door. The problem is that the advisor is going to give the retiree the same advice he gave the twenty-, thirty-, and forty-year-old. In other words, the advisor is a general practitioner.

Your general practitioner may be a great doctor, but they are likely not the only doctor you will ever need. One of the advisors in our office tells a story about his father-in-law, Frank. Frank worked at General Motors for thirty years, and when he retired he found that he really missed staying busy with work. He went back to work as a delivery driver for ten to fifteen years. Once that got to be too tough on his body, he got a job at the local hospital in his small town, working in the receiving department.

As we all know, life happens, and after working at the hospital for a few years, Frank started having chest pains. Where do you think he went to get those pains checked out? That exact hospital, of course. He personally knew the staff and was happy to place his trust in them. After they ran tests on Frank's heart, they advised that he needed major heart surgery to fix the blockage, and they scheduled it for the very next week.

Frank's wife and kids were extremely worried about the prospect of open-heart surgery and pleaded with him to get a second opinion. He eventually gave in and went to a heart and vascular hospital in the nearest big city. After looking over all of Frank's tests, they let him know that a stent would take care of the problem. This meant he would need an angioplasty procedure, not open-heart surgery!

The small-town hospital doctors wanted to open Frank up so they would have clear access to the trouble spot of his heart. The heart and vascular hospital doctors are specialists. They do these procedures three to five times a day, as opposed to just a few times a month, so they were much more confident that Frank only needed a stent.

As you get closer to retirement, you need to make sure you work with a retirement specialist who works with similar-aged people every day. They've seen the concerns and problems and have been able to give appropriate guidance, a blueprint if you will, to their clients.

This is a journey, and we've taken many, many people on this journey before you—and have been successful doing it.

Happiness and peace of mind await you, knowing your money is secure and in good hands. You will be able to explore new hobbies and reconnect with your family.

Remember: it's not the beginning of the end; it's a new beginning.

> "Knowledge is power, but execution trumps knowledge, so it's what you do from here that will matter."
>
> —TONY ROBBINS

A FINAL WORD ABOUT OUR RETIRE TOGETHER PROGRAM

Retire Together connects retirees who have similar interests, such as traveling, golfing, painting, gardening, swing dancing, hiking, biking, and more. As many retirees discover, leaving one life to begin another can sometimes be challenging. Loneliness can set in. They miss the camaraderie they had on the job. They want to meet others with whom they can enjoy shared activities, chat about their weekend, and more.

Toward that end, we have events a few times a year where our clients are able to get together, meet each other, network, and become friends. Outside of these events, we also have a Retire Together online portal where our clients are able to stay connected and share what they have been up to lately in retirement.

A few of our clients got the idea for Retire Together after attending our annual Christmas celebration. Who would have known they had already booked the same trip on a cruise ship to Antarctica? Yes, that's right, totally coincidentally they had wound up on the same trip and ended up getting to know one another while cruising from Buenos Aires to Antarctica and then back to South America, where they spent time in Chile. Now, they travel together all over the world and are always looking for other couples to join them on their adventures.

These clients are living proof that retirement can be so much more than just a period of your life that you "get through" while worrying about your money. In fact, it can be the most fun and exciting time you've ever had!

CONCLUSION

DON'T LIVE TO WORK,
WORK TO LIVE

My grandmother, Nora Slagle, ran a restaurant in my home-town of Winchester, Illinois, for over fifty years. She worked six and a half days a week, from 5:30 a.m. until 9:00 p.m. The only break she ever got was for an hour each after-noon, from 3:00 to 4:00 p.m., which was when she would go home to watch her favorite show, *Days of Our Lives*.

She finally decided to retire at seventy-four years of age. After retirement, however, she didn't know what to do with her time. She had no hobbies. Her only "hobby" had always been working.

But, eventually, she found a hobby in her retirement years.

She decided to devote her time to taking care of other elderly people in their homes. She did this until she passed away at age eighty-five.

These days, I try to live by what I learned from my grandmother and always have things I enjoy doing outside of work. No matter how busy you are, make sure you find time to do what makes you happy, whether it is traveling, gardening, exercising, spending time with grandkids, or something else.

> Make sure you aren't living to work; you must work so you can live.

Don't wait for the "right time." The time is now!

No matter what situation you find yourself in—whether you're counting down to retirement, close to retirement, or already living the retired life—just remember that **you are defined not by the job you do but by the person you are.**

And regardless of what phase of life you are in, you should be living your best life each and every day!

ACKNOWLEDGMENTS

This book would not have been possible without the time, talents, and patience of Samantha Martin. She kept me on track with deadlines and weekly meetings, which is no easy task.

In addition, I would like to thank Chad Tobin, Sarah Newton, and the rest of the team at Slagle Financial for helping me build one of the top retirement firms in the country.

I would also like to thank my parents, Ron and Linda Slagle, for giving me the life lessons to be the man I am today.

And finally, thanks to all of our wonderful clients, who trust us to guide them on this ever-changing journey to and through retirement.

ABOUT THE AUTHOR

CHAD SLAGLE grew up in a small Illinois farm town and learned the value of hard work at an early age. This strong work ethic helped Chad play college football, coach high-school football for ten years, and start his own financial firm out of the back of his truck. Chad draws from the techniques and ideologies he learned coaching football and uses those every day as the president and founder of Slagle Financial, which has seven offices across Illinois and Missouri. He's the host of *The Chad Slagle Show: Coaching You to and through Retirement*, which airs on ABC, NBC, and CBS affiliates throughout Illinois and Missouri. Chad lives in Edwardsville, Illinois, with his wife and four children.

CPSIA information can be obtained
at www.ICGtesting.com
Printed in the USA
BVHW041511081122
650437BV00006B/10/J

9 781544 506968